ME AND
MY SENSES

ME AND MY SENSES

by Joan Sweeney   illustrated by Annette Cable

SCHOLASTIC INC.

New York Toronto London Auckland Sydney
Mexico City New Delhi Hong Kong Buenos Aires

For our latest sensation, Liam
—J.S.

In memory of Mom
love, A.C.

ISBN 0-439-70729-3

Text copyright © 2003 by Joan Sweeney. Illustrations copyright © 2003 by Annette Cable.
All rights reserved. Published by Scholastic Inc., 557 Broadway, New York, NY 10012,
by arrangement with Random House Children's Books, a division of Random House, Inc.
SCHOLASTIC and associated logos are trademarks and/or registered trademarks of Scholastic Inc.

12 11 10 9 8 7 6   6 7 8 9 10/0

Printed in the U.S.A.   40

First Scholastic printing, January 2005

This is me. Guess what I'm having for lunch?
Let's use my five senses to find out!

I see a van out in front.
I **see** with my eyes.

This box feels warm to my touch. I **touch** with my hands.

PIZZA

Thank you, sir!

I smell something good. I **smell** with my nose.

"Mmmmmmm!"

PIZZA

I taste what's inside. I **taste** with my tongue.

My five senses are hearing, seeing, touching, smelling, and tasting.

Each sense works in a different way to send messages to my brain. All together they tell me the delicious news: we're having pizza for lunch!

hearing

Sound waves vibrate through my ears so I can hear.

M)))

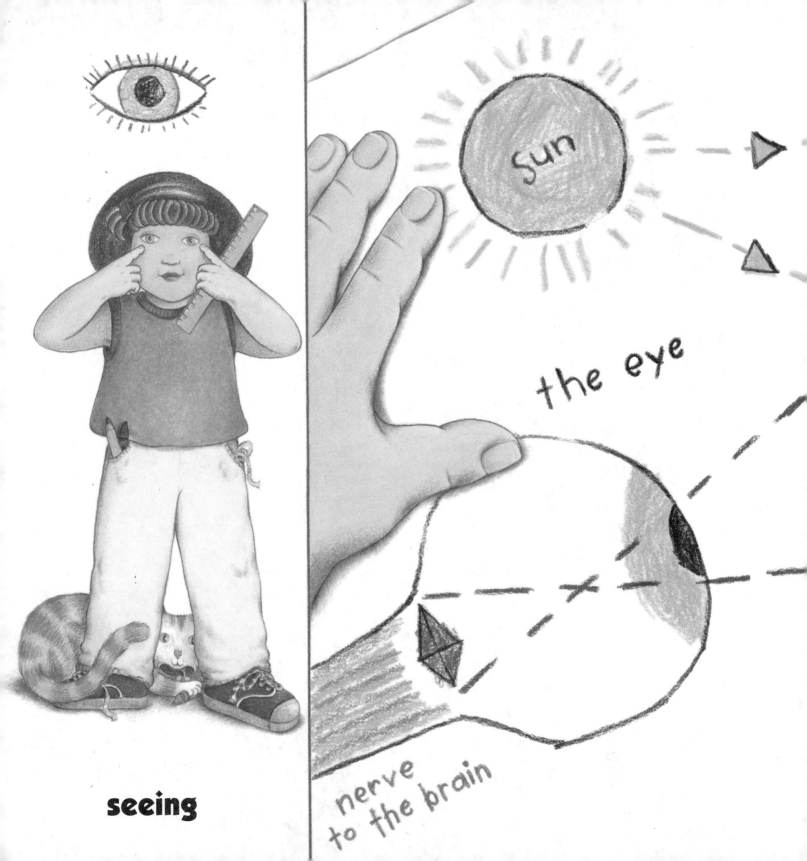

seeing

Sun

the eye

nerve to the brain

Kite

Light rays bounce off an object and send
a picture to my brain so I can see.

touching

Special cells in my skin tell me what's hot, cold, soft, itchy, heavy, or painful when I touch.

smelling

Over five million smell cells inside my nose tell
me what's a skunk or a flower when I smell.

tasting

Tiny taste buds on my tongue tell
me if something is sweet, sour, salty,
or bitter when I taste.

Sometimes I use just
one of my senses.

I smell brownies
baking.

I hear Daddy
whistle.

I see my book
with the help
of a flashlight.

I taste salty
crackers.

I feel cold
ice cubes.

Sometimes I use all my senses at once. I see dark clouds above while I hear thunder rumble. I feel raindrops fall and I can taste them on my tongue....

I smell the wet grass. It smells fresh and good.

Because I hear, see, touch, smell, and taste, the world makes a whole lot more sense!

Things I Can Do With My Five Senses:

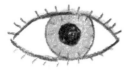 see:

 hear: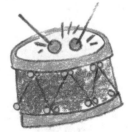

 touch:

 **smell:**

 **taste:**

Make a list of your own!